The <u>Mackenzie Meets Alzheimer's Disease Picture Book</u> is an Alzheimer's awareness book that is the perfect introduction to Alzheimer's disease for young children. EnJOY reading, following along while listening to the downloadable song, and singing as you read the book.

Link to download the song:
https://www.mackenziemeetsalzheimers.com/pl/2147653083

Visit https://www.MackenzieMeetsAlzheimers.com/
and learn about the components in the
<u>Mackenzie Meets Alzheimer's Awareness Program</u>.

The Program is a toolkit for interacting with a loved one who has Alzheimer's disease, or any type of dementia. The videos in the Program provide activities for children and families to help create positive memories with their loved one from diagnosis through the severe stage.

Your gift for purchasing this book is 50% off the <u>Mackenzie Meets Alzheimer's Awareness Program</u>.

Go to the website, scroll down and purchase the Program that best fits your needs.
Use the discount code **MMAAP50**
when you check out.

This **Mackenzie Meets Alzheimer's Disease Picture Book** is a component of the **Mackenzie Meets Alzheimer's Awareness Program**.

The educational video series in the Mackenzie Meets Alzheimer's Awareness Program is a gift to families who have loved ones with Alzheimer's disease and children who are experiencing the changes in, for example, their grandparents. The Program equips children and the responsible adults 'sandwiched' between caring for their children and their loved one to responsibly navigate the disease.

For children, it's a valuable blend of the following: Alzheimer's education offered at a level they can understand; suggestions for activities families can do together with the loved one who has the disease; being open about the challenges of the disease; giving children permission to feel emotions including anger, fear, confusion and sadness, and helping them appropriately express those emotions. The graphics in the videos beautifully reflect the information presented.

The video for the responsible adult is powerful! It's filled with education as well as detailed examples for how they can provide family Alzheimer's support for both the loved one with Alzheimer's disease AND their children.

The Quick Reference Guide is a great bonus. It's a high-level summary of key points from the videos including tips for interacting with the person who has Alzheimer's disease, and tips for talking with children about the disease. As Mackenzie Meets Alzheimer's explains: "Refer to this guide to help you understand the behavior of a person with Alzheimer's disease, help your child understand that person, and easily access fun activities for your child (and you) to do to successfully interact and maintain a relationship with that person."

The animated video for early readers is a fun children's video creatively and beautifully designed to introduce them to the disease, what they may experience, and to feel love throughout the journey. The artwork is great and the music is engaging. I was tremendously impressed with how the story song shared with honesty about the disease, wove love through all of it, and helped the 'monster' of Alzheimer's disease be less scary. I watched the video several times. It can easily be broken down into small segments for children to watch a little at a time – well done.

Sue Ryan, TEDx, MS, ICF, NLP, ILEC, 3-time international best-selling author, Caregiving Industry Influencer

Moondance Treasures Music Publishing

Mackenzie Meets Alzheimer's Disease Picture Book
Text & Illustrations copyright © 2022 by Alder Allensworth & Brenda Freed
All rights reserved.
No part of this book may be used or reproduced in any manner whatsoever without written permission except in the case of brief quotations embodied in critical articles and reviews.

Downloadable Mackenzie Meets Alzheimer's Disease Story Song copyright © 2020 (BMI)
Lyrics by Alder Allensworth & Brenda Freed
Music by Brenda Freed

For information address:
Moondance Treasures Music Publishing
204 Walnut Springs Lane
Stonewall, TX 78671
Email: MackenzieMeetsAlzheimers@gmail.com
https://www.MackenzieMeetsAlzheimers.com

Library of Congress Control Number: 2023907785
ISBN 979-8-218-19792-6

**In memory of
Chad Dickey, PhD
for dedicating his life to finding a cure for Alzheimer's disease**

Mackenzie Meets Alzheimer's Disease Picture Book

text by
Alder Allensworth & Brenda Freed

illustrations by
William Banda

When I feel scared or when I'm sick, my dear Gran sings to me

the Agape song, which makes me feel safe and so at peace.

I feel the love between us,
and I know I'll make it through

the fear, the aches and pains I'm feeling from that thonky flu.

Agape, Agape, be well and sing with me.
Agape, Agape, means love for you and me.

When a storm is near
and I'm afraid to go to bed,

the lightning and the thunder make me want to hide my head.

With paper and her markers,
my Gran comes to my side.

We quiet down my fears
and draw a monster we call "Sunshine."

Agape, Agape, now I can go to sleep.
Agape, Agape, means love for you and me.

I always love to visit Gran on holidays from school.

The lake, the garden
and the waterfall are very cool.

She likes to sing and dance
the Agape song with me.

We go to see the butterflies and watch them flying free.

Agape, Agape, sing and dance with me.
Agape, Agape, means love for you and me.

Now Mom and Dad are telling me my Gran is not so well.

I'm not sure what she'll be like,
or what I can do to help.

A disease called Alzheimer's is making her act strange.

It's making things go really wrong
in my dear Gran's brain.

Agape, Agape, I wonder what Gran needs.
Agape, Agape, means love for you and me.

Alzheimer's makes Gran feel thonky and forget a lot of things.

Sometimes she feels real scared
and sometimes hides her diamond ring.

Now and then she sleeps all day and wanders through the night.

And when she leaves the burner on, it gives us such a fright. Oh!

Agape, Agape, help my Gran, oh please.
Agape, Agape, means love for you and me.

Dad says you can't get Alzheimer's like you catch the flu.

He says Gran may act angry
and won't play like she used to do.

And Gran now has a walker
to help keep her on her feet.

She wears a safety bracelet with her address and I.D.

Agape, Agape, keep Gran safe, oh please.
Agape, Agape, means love for you and me.

Some people get Alzheimer's as they're growing old.

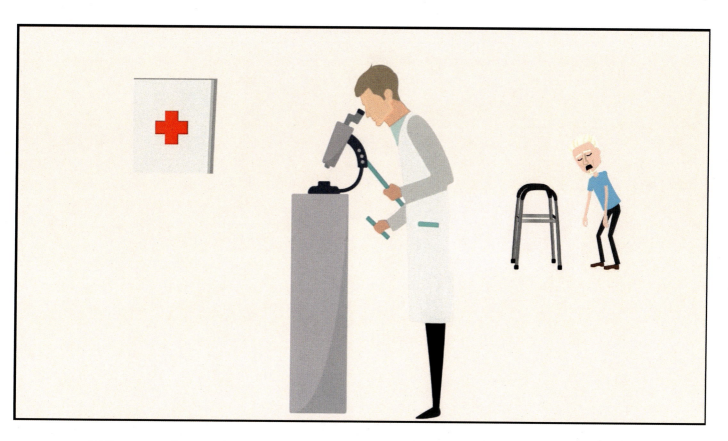

The doctors haven't found a cure
but they're getting close I'm told.

I'll draw a monster, call her Tiny.
She will be my scout.

She'll help me help my Gran.
She'll help me figure it all out.

Agape, Agape, help is near you'll see.
Agape, Agape, means love for you and me.

So Tiny told me what to draw.
Agape monster's here

to help my Gran and chase away all her thonky fears.

My Gran can still sing and dance and laugh so joyfully.

But Alzheimer's is weird
and she might not remember me.

Agape, Agape, Alzheimer's can't scare me.
Agape, Agape, means love for you and me.

The Agape monster and a song,
I will share with you.

So you can help your own Grandma,
or your Grandpa, too.

Love and understanding are the only things we need

to help us cope with Alzheimer's,
that thonky disease.

Agape, Agape, love is all we need.
Agape, Agape, means love for you and me.

Agape, Agape, love is all we need.
Agape, Agape, means love for you and me.

about the authors

Alder Allensworth
Alder Allensworth, MM, RN, is a registered nurse and has a Master's degree in Music Therapy. The inspiration for this project came from Allensworth's personal experience watching her Mother, who had Alzheimer's disease, interact with the grandchildren. Professionally, she worked with children and geriatrics, including those with Alzheimer's disease. Allensworth has also published several articles in professional journals. She won a Richter Publishing book contract in 2017. Her book, Prevail: Celebrate the Journey, is available on Amazon and has a five star review rating. She is a speaker and presenter in the field of disabilities on local, national and international stages. Allensworth has been featured on CNN, local and international television and newspapers for her life's work of promoting quality of life for people of all abilities.

Brenda Freed
Brenda Freed, MA, has a Master's degree in Music Education/Music Therapy, with an emphasis in counseling. Freed pioneered the Music Therapy Program at the University of Iowa Hospitals and Clinics where she worked with patients of all ages and diagnoses, including Alzheimer's disease. She has published music therapy articles, a poetry magazine and an arts and entertainment magazine. Freed teaches voice, piano and guitar online to all ages, voice and harmony workshops at festivals and conferences, and has produced a line of Effortless Music Instruction Products. She created the Young Artist Performance Incubator (YAPI) program at the renowned Kerrville Folk Festival. Freed is also a performing singer songwriter with several published albums of original material. She and her husband perform as Him & Her TX.

Made in the USA
Columbia, SC
23 June 2023